Postcard History Series

# Clyde

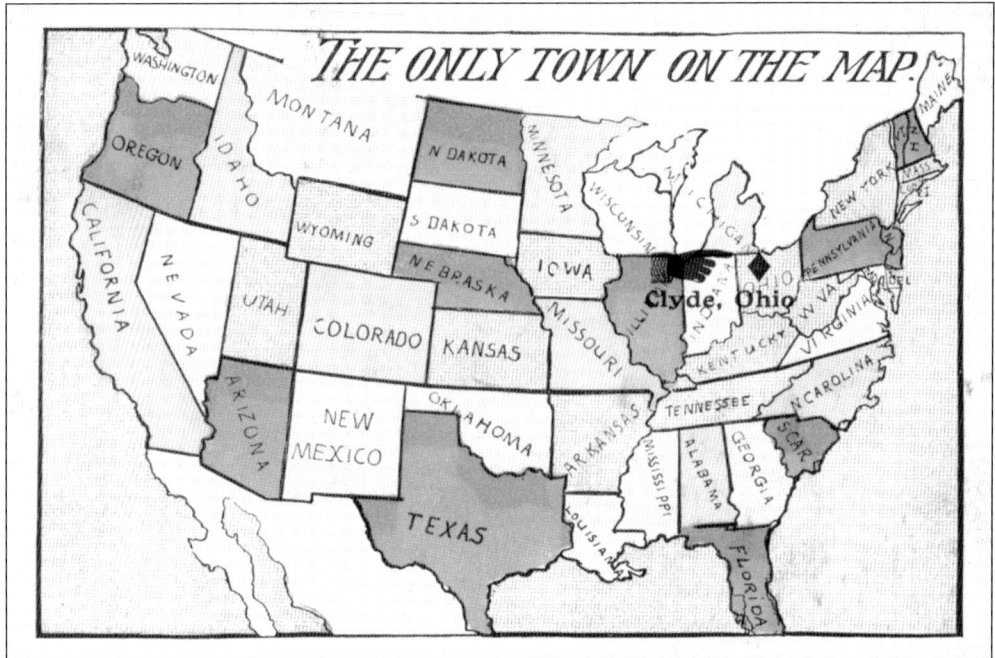

A promotional postcard printed in approximately 1910 points to Clyde, Ohio, as "the only town on the map." The postcard not only places the city of Clyde geographically, it also provides a window into an era of postcard popularity. (John Sanford.)

**On the Front Cover:** This postcard view of Clyde's Main Street looks south from the railroad tracks toward the intersection with Maple Street; it shows a vibrant and bustling downtown in the early 20th century. (John Sanford.)

**On the Back Cover:** This undated postcard shows a track meet that took place at the fairgrounds in Clyde with a track team from nearby Sandusky, Ohio. The fairgrounds were located on the present-day site of Community Park. (John Sanford.)

# Postcard History Series

# Clyde

*Tiffany Willey Middleton*
*Foreword by Gene A. Smith*

Copyright © 2017 by Tiffany Willey Middleton
ISBN 978-1-4671-2670-0

Published by Arcadia Publishing
Charleston, South Carolina

Printed in the United States of America

Library of Congress Control Number: 2017932816

For all general information contact Arcadia Publishing at:
Telephone 843-853-2070
Fax 843-853-0044
E-mail sales@arcadiapublishing.com
For customer service and orders:
Toll-Free 1-888-313-2665

Visit us on the Internet at www.arcadiapublishing.com

*To everyone in Clyde who collects or is inspired by old postcards;
and to Jonas and Abigail, always steadfast cheerleaders.*

# Contents

Foreword 6

Acknowledgments 7

Introduction 8

1. A "Famous Small Town" 11
2. A Great Place to Live 23
3. A Great Place to Work 41
4. A Great Place to Visit 69
5. All Around the Town 85
6. A Walk Down Main Street 103

Index 126

About the Clyde Museum 127

# Foreword

*Deltiology* is a word that is probably uncommon to many people, but it is a term that refers to the collection and study of postcards. Collecting postcards is considered one of the largest global collecting hobbies, surpassed only by collecting coins and stamps. The popularity of collecting postcards can be ascribed to a variety of factors, most notably their subjects, which can be almost anything. Postcards are available in most parts of the world. They are probably one of the most popular forms of souvenirs bought by travelers and have been a primary means of staying in contact with family and friends while traveling. They may be mailed with low-cost postage, offering a snapshot of one's environs while traveling to anyone else in the world.

Postcards offer great value and significance to researchers and enthusiasts who are interested in the iconography of communities, regions, and indigenous peoples. Postcards are preserved by museums, libraries, historical societies, genealogical societies, archives, and individuals because of their importance in research. They freeze in time how a community, businesses, schools, and other organizations looked, and they provide a reference point to show how they have changed over time. They can show how people dressed, lived, worked, and experienced their communities. Postcards also became an economical means of advertising for businesses and various types of organizations. Postcards are much more than just a pretty picture on a card—they are glimpses into our past that exhibit how we have changed as a people and a society both domestically and globally. This book shows how people dressed, lived, and worked in Clyde, Ohio, and provides a window into how our town has evolved over time into the very American community that it is today.

—Gene A. Smith
Curator, Clyde Museum

# Acknowledgments

This postcard history about Clyde, Ohio, is the result of a team of generous librarians, archivists, researchers, and collectors who all lent their help and encouragement—and postcards—to me for this project. They all deserve thanks. Thank-yous go to the postcard providers: the Clyde Museum and private collectors/Clyde residents Randy Dick, John Sanford, and Paula Renfro. Thank-yous go to Gene A. Smith at the Clyde Museum, Brenda Stultz, and the Clyde Heritage League for supporting the project. After Randy, John, and Paula opened their postcard collections, Jill McCullough, then at the Clyde Public Library, scanned them all so that they could be digitized, shared, and workable for this project.

A thank-you goes to Dorothy Cox for providing immensely helpful initial research about practically every postcard she touched and writing it all down for me. I could hear her voice as I read her notes, and that was simply wonderful. Thanks go to Lynn Monday for managing Dorothy's research, providing additional images, and answering so many questions. Additional thanks go to the Clyde Public Library, Nan Card and the Hayes Presidential Library and Museums, Lily Burkheimer and the Ohio History Connection, and James Semon.

Several digital archives were used to research captions in this book and, in some cases, provided public domain images and quotable quotes. The archive of the *Clyde Enterprise*; Clyde city directories from 1887, 1908, and 1913; the City of Clyde's list of McPherson Cemetery interments; the catalog at "Old Ohio Schools"; the database of the Library of Congress, and histories available through archiving giants Internet Archive and Google Books all proved invaluable. Certain published local histories served as resources; they are *Twentieth Century History of Sandusky County, Ohio and Representative Citizens*, by Basil Meek, published in 1909; *A History of Northwest Ohio*, volumes I, II, and III, by Nevin Winter, published in 1917; and *These Things Stay By You*, published in 1966 by the Whirlpool Corporation.

Final thanks go to everyone at Arcadia Publishing, for answering questions, offering help and edits, and generally encouraging me to keep this project on track.

# Introduction

This is a book about Clyde, Ohio. Clyde is a community located in northwest Ohio less than one hour southeast of Toledo and two hours northwest of Columbus. At the time of the 2010 census, the city's population was approximately 6,300 people. This is also a book of postcards, the distinctive pieces of mail that appear in mailboxes around the world and have come to inspire collectors. Most of the postcards in this book span a time period between 1900 and 1960 and provide a window into the buildings, homes, and everyday life in Clyde during the first half of the 20th century.

The city of Clyde was incorporated as a village in 1866. The first documented settler was Jesse Benton, who settled on land in the present-day city limits in 1820. In 1827, the Western Reserve and Maumee Pike (now US Route 20 or McPherson Highway) was built as an early road in Clyde. Clyde first developed as "Hamer's Corners" along this route at its present-day intersection with Maple Street. It was named after William Hamer, who operated a tavern or hotel—or both—at the intersection. The name *Clyde* was adopted in 1852 after being proposed by O.P. Woodward, who had lived in Clyde, New York, which was named after the famous Clyde river and valley in Scotland. That same year, the first railroad lines were built in Clyde. Two lines intersected slightly west of Hamer's Corners near the present-day intersection of Main and Railroad Streets. Soon, hotels, a stagecoach service, and Clyde's downtown developed around the railroad. The rail lines—the Toledo & Norwalk Railway (later the Lake Shore & Michigan Southern line) and the Sandusky City & Indiana Railway (later the Cleveland, Cincinnati, Chicago, and St. Louis, or "Big Four" line)—connected the city to the rest of the country and facilitated national and global trade options for local manufacturers. By 1900, when the postcards in this book began to appear, Clyde was a vibrant community with homes, schools, manufacturers and businesses, hotels, and entertainment venues. The 1908 city directory promises:

> We have good homes, good churches of the leading denominations, progressive schools of increasing efficiency, a magnificent Carnegie Public Library, a new State Armory, a well established lyceum course and various religions, fraternal, literary and philanthropic organizations that minister well to the higher needs of our community life.

At that time, Clyde's population was approximately 3,000, which the city directory describes as "a people classed neither as rich nor poor, but mainly as thrifty, prosperous citizens, producing for the community, providing for their families, and enjoying life under pleasant environment." The postcards in this book showcase the community described in the 1908 city directory and show how it evolved over the next 50 years.

Postcards really started to appear in the United States in 1861, after Congress authorized postal legislation that allowed privately printed cards weighing one ounce or less to be sent in the mail. That year, John Charlton copyrighted the first postcard in the United States. Souvenir postcards were popular at events like the 1893 World's Fair, which inspired collectors, if not senders. It was 1907, however, when the postcards modern people recognize really began booming in popularity. That year, Congress authorized the "split back" on postcards, which allowed for space for a note on the left side and for a mailing address and postage on the right side. Prior to this authorization, only the mailing address and postage could be included on the back of a postcard, so any note to the recipient had to be written across the image or in the margins on the front side.

This simple change helped to launch what historians and collectors recognize as the "Golden Age of Postcards." In 1908, the US Post Office processed 700 million postcards; in 1913, that number increased to 900 million. This golden age extended to approximately 1915, when World War I led to a decrease in postcard mailing. After the war, the mailing of postcards picked up again, but it never reached the same popularity as during that earlier time period.

Much of the ubiquity of postcards stems from their subject matter: anything. In addition to mass-produced printed designs, postcards became as easy to print as modern-day personal photographs, and in many cases, they were modern photographs. In 1907, Kodak introduced the real-photo postcard and offered a service that allowed film to be printed on postcard stock. Real-photo postcards became incredibly popular, as anyone with a camera could print and mail them. Professional postcard photographers documented anything they thought people might want to remember. Postcard historian Fred Bassett explains, "Whenever America paraded or celebrated anything, the postcard photographer was there. He was also there when disasters—fires, floods, earthquakes, train wrecks—occurred." The practice of documenting even the worst aspects of society on a postcard was not uncommon. In his 1965 song "Desolation Row," Bob Dylan sings, "They're selling postcards of the hanging" in reference to postcards that were printed following a lynching in Duluth, Minnesota, in 1920. Postcards became a medium for documenting the extraordinary, the newsworthy, and the everyday. Everyone mailed them—from the rich and famous to the poor and anonymous.

However, postcards were more than their images; they were a leap into the 20th-century world of wider mass communication in much the same way that social media is today. Suddenly, anyone could share a photograph or image with anyone else simply by dropping a card in the mail. Critics saw the culture of communication changing and bemoaned the decline of the letter in favor of a postcard. They also remarked on the use of abbreviations, which became increasingly common as people squeezed greetings onto the small cards. This line of complaint was not so different from contemporary ruminations on the effects of abbreviated communications in texting or social media. Postcards also had an "instant" quality about them and appeared more dynamic—and sometimes even more elegant—than a letter, because they presented the recipient with an image in addition to text.

The postcards of Clyde featured in this book are organized into six chapters. The first chapter covers famous subjects, including James B. McPherson and McPherson Cemetery, as well as some of the lesser-known famous folks who passed through Clyde, including orator Emma Lemon. Edward Payson Weston, a nationally known "professional pedestrian," traveled through Clyde in 1910 on a walk from Maine to Chicago, and someone took a photograph and made a postcard.

Chapters 2 through 4 showcase postcards related to "living," "working," and "visiting" in Clyde. Chapter 2 deals with living in Clyde and features views of homes and streets in the city, as well as residents. An image in that chapter shows that Buckeye Street, while it looks much the same as it did a century ago, also looks dramatically different in some parts.

Chapter 3 features postcard views of people at work and their workplaces in Clyde. This chapter shows that Clyde was once an automobile manufacturing center. The Elmore Manufacturing Company, Krebs Commercial Car Company, and Clydesdale Motor Truck Company all occupied factory space in the city. The chapter also illustrates that Clyde was once world-famous for sauerkraut processing and stone-monument design. The origins of Clyde's largest current employer, Whirlpool, are shown in the buildings of Universal Paper Products, Vitrified Iron, and Davidson Enamel.

Chapter 4 highlights the hotels and tourist camps that visitors frequented. Postcard views of the railroad depot and interurban station are included—trains stopped in Clyde more than a dozen times each day to offer residents transportation to nearby cities.

Chapter 5 is titled "All Around the Town" and includes postcard views of schools and school events and subjects such as churches, Waterworks Pond, and Harkness Theater. The Clyde Public Library, then new, shines as a prized community resource, much as it remains today. Local clubs, including the Camp Fire organization, Buckeye Club basketball team, and city baseball clubs are also showcased.

The final chapter, chapter 6, features Main Street. Titled "A Walk Down Main Street," the chapter begins with postcard views north of downtown and progresses south down the street. In addition to moving geographically down the street, these views also move through time. Despite its transition from horse-drawn wagons to cars, Main Street in Clyde looks much the same—yet also very different—to longtime residents or frequent visitors.

The images presented in this book came from a variety of sources, primarily the Clyde Museum and several local private collectors. Each image includes a courtesy line at the end of the caption that provides clear documentation. The people and locations in the images have been identified to the extent that they were known or able to be researched. This means that even when there are unidentified persons and locations shown in these postcards, based on one clue or another, the postcard relates to Clyde. Likewise, if there is a date on a postcard, it is noted in its caption.

Across all of the postcards, there is a comfortable familiarity with these moments from Clyde history; things look similar, or maybe readers will remember certain people, places, or things. There is also a sense of a different time—perhaps even a bygone era—as certain long-gone features around the city are shown, and readers may consider how they helped to shape the community of Clyde as it is today. In these ways, this tour through postcards of Clyde might bring back memories or teach readers something new about Clyde history.

In any event, whether you live in, work in, or visit Clyde, hopefully you will be inspired by the stories presented across these chapters.

# One

# A "Famous Small Town"

McPherson Cemetery, located at the corner of McPherson Highway and East Maple Street, is Clyde's most storied cemetery. It was named after Clyde native Gen. James B. McPherson (1828–1864), the second-highest-ranking Union officer killed during the Civil War, who is buried there alongside his mother and father. His grave is marked with a bronze statue. The cemetery land was once part of a 150-acre farm owned by Albert Guinall (1823–1852). As the story goes, Albert's wife, Nellie, became ill and pointed to the hill where the statue now stands and requested, "Let me be carried there." Albert fenced off a plot around the hill, which became a small cemetery. Nellie recovered, but the Guinalls were eventually buried there, and the area became known as Evergreen Cemetery. It became a public cemetery for the growing city of Clyde in 1868. In this postcard view, the cemetery looks tranquil after a fresh snow on February 14, 1909. The statue of General McPherson is visible through the trees. (Randy Dick.)

James Birdseye McPherson was born in Clyde in 1828 to William R. and Cynthia Russell McPherson. The McPherson home still stands in Clyde at the corner of Maple Street and McPherson Highway. McPherson attended the nearby Norwalk Academy and graduated from the US Military Academy at West Point in 1853. He spent his career in the military, initially with the Corps of Engineers overseeing projects along the Hudson River in New York and at Alcatraz Island in San Francisco. During the Civil War, McPherson was promoted to general and given command of Union army commander Ulysses S. Grant's Army of Tennessee. McPherson was killed during the Battle of Atlanta on July 22, 1864. He was the second-highest-ranking Union officer to die during the war. He was buried in what was then known as Evergreen Cemetery; it was rededicated as McPherson Cemetery in his honor in 1881. This photograph of McPherson was taken by famed Civil War photographer Mathew Brady sometime between 1862 and 1864. (Library of Congress.)

A bronze statue in McPherson Cemetery marks the grave of James B. McPherson. It was designed by Louis Rebisso (1839–1899), of Cincinnati, Ohio, and was paid for by the people of Clyde and surrounding Sandusky County and other Civil War veterans. They worked for over a decade to raise the necessary funds. The statue depicts McPherson standing with his weaponry and binoculars and pointing north. His foot rests on a cannon, while cannonballs sit at the base of the statue. The memorial was dedicated on July 22, 1881. It was reported that over 10,000 people attended the event. Pres. Rutherford B. Hayes eulogized the general during the dedication: "His name will be forever found on the shining roll of the world's best-loved heroes." Other ceremony attendees included Cynthia McPherson, the general's mother, and Gen. William Tecumseh Sherman, who served with McPherson during the Civil War. (Randy Dick.)

The iron gates that frame the entrance to McPherson Cemetery were installed in 1901. The entrance to the cemetery was moved to its current position from Maple Street at the end of the 19th century. After the dedication of the McPherson statue in 1881, the cemetery continued to grow. In 1897, Clyde city officials hired Cleveland landscape architect Arthur Babcox to beautify the cemetery and make it more like a park. This undated postcard shows the cemetery on a sunny day during the 20th century. Note the expansive green space and tall trees in the cemetery, as well as the detailed columns and fencing that surround it. In the foreground of the postcard, outside of the cemetery gates, brick pavers span McPherson Highway. (Randy Dick.)

Political cartoonist James Albert Wales (1852–1886) was buried in McPherson Cemetery. He was born in Clyde and became a nationally known caricaturist. He drew cartoons for popular magazines of the 19th century, including *Puck* and *Harper's Weekly*, and was one of the founders of *Judge*. Wales was the first native-born American political cartoonist to achieve national notoriety. When he died in 1886, the *New York Times* ran his obituary. An example of his work includes this cover illustration for the July 13, 1881, issue of *Puck*. The cartoon depicts Charles Guiteau, who was convicted of assassinating Pres. James Garfield. Guiteau felt largely responsible for Garfield's election and was disgruntled after not receiving a presidential appointment among the Garfield administration. The cartoon shows him holding a note, "An office or your life!" while standing outside of the White House ready to ring the "president's bell." (Library of Congress.)

This granite statue of George Burton Meek (1872–1898) stands inside McPherson Cemetery to mark the grave of Meek, who is believed to have been the first American serviceman killed during the Spanish-American War. He was born in nearby Riley Township and enlisted in the US Navy in 1892. Fireman First Class Meek was killed aboard the torpedo boat USS *Winslow* at Cardenas, Cuba, on May 11, 1898. He was buried in McPherson Cemetery in 1899 after a parade in his honor through downtown Clyde. The State of Ohio erected the memorial, which was dedicated by Ohio governor Frank Willis on May 11, 1916. The statue stands 13 feet tall and was designed and produced locally by the Hughes Granite Company. (Randy Dick.)

There are over 13,000 people interred at McPherson Cemetery, including city leaders, longtime residents, and other influential persons. Notable burials include Benjamin Collins (d. 1825), the first constable of Green Creek Township; Charles Henry McCleary (d. 1906), who was awarded the Congressional Medal of Honor for his service during the Civil War; local merchant Alonzo Wilder (d. 1912); Sarah Suggitt (d. 1932), a local high school teacher who gifted $3,500 to friends who established a fund at the Clyde Public Library in her honor to buy books for the community; former mayor and local businessman Winfield Adare (d. 1932); Silas Richards (d. 1946), a local judge who was instrumental in securing funding to build the Clyde Public Library; local artist Franklyn Hall (d. 1965); and local architect and historian Thaddeus Hurd (d. 1989). (Above, Clyde Museum; below, Randy Dick.)

One of McPherson Cemetery's most renowned "residents" is Rodger Young, who died in 1943 during World War II after putting himself in harm's way to allow other members of his platoon to withdraw from enemy fire. His actions were immortalized in the song "The Ballad of Rodger Young," by Frank Loesser. He was posthumously awarded the Medal of Honor, the United States' highest military honor. Young was born in Tiffin, Ohio, in 1918, and lived in nearby Green Springs before moving to Clyde. He enlisted in the Ohio National Guard in 1938. In 1942, Young's unit was deployed to Fiji, then the Solomon Islands, then New Georgia. There, on July 31, 1943, Young's platoon was ambushed by Japanese soldiers as they were returning to camp. With everyone under enemy fire and some injuries, the platoon was ordered to withdraw. Young continued to proceed, which allowed him opportunities to inflict casualties and allowed his fellow soldiers time to escape. He was initially buried on New Georgia, but in 1949, his body was returned to the United States and buried in Clyde. (Ohio History Connection.)

# "ELI PERKINS, At Large.

## HIS TALK

At _Terry's Hall_ in _Clyde O_ - Jan. _13th_ 1880.

**ADMIT the BEARER or WIFE,** His own wife,

FOR YEARS AND YEARS.

Seat No. _27_ .... Sec. _G_ ... Row ... _6_ ...

The Lecturer will commence at 8 o'clock, sharp, and continue 'till somebody requests him to stop.

In case of an accident to the lecturer, or if he should die or be hung before the evening of the disturbance, this ticket will admit the bearer to a front seat at the funeral, where he can sit and enjoy himself the same as at the lecture.

*The highest priced seats, those nearest the door, are reserved for the particular friends of the speaker.*

(Retain this Coupon for your seat.) [PLEASE DON'T TURN OVER]

Eli Perkins was the pen name and stage name of humorist lecturer Melville DeLancey Landon (1839–1910). He was from New York, served in the Union army during the Civil War, and appeared at Terry's Hall in Clyde on January 13, 1880. The city directory from 1887 lists Terry's Hall, or Terry's Opera House, as located at 106–110 South Main Street, which is where the Clyde–Green Springs School Board office is now located. (Randy Dick.)

Emma D. Lemon was a professional orator who traveled around the country performing dramatic readings, primarily from 1893 until 1897. This postcard advertises her "grand elocutionary and dramatic entertainment" for an appearance in Clyde on November 15, 1883. She was a graduate of the Boston School of Oratory (now known as Emerson College) in Boston. The *Elyria Republican*, the local newspaper from nearby Elyria, Ohio, reviewed one of her performances: "It is surprising how enjoyable and instructive reading can be." (Randy Dick.)

Two of Clyde's most prominent natives are brothers Karl and Sherwood Anderson. Karl Anderson became a respected artist. In 1919, Sherwood published *Winesburg, Ohio: A Group of Tales of Ohio Small-Town Life*, a significant composite novel. Irwin and Emma Anderson moved their family to Clyde in 1884. The Anderson children are pictured in this 1886 studio photograph. They are, from left to right: (seated) Irwin (1878–1934), Ray (1883–1946), Earl (1885–1927), and Sherwood (1876–1941); (standing) Karl (1874–1956) and Stella (1875–1917). The Anderson family left Clyde after Emma's death in 1895. (Ohio Historical Society.)

Members of the 72nd Ohio Volunteer Infantry (O.V.I.), which served in the Civil War, attended an annual reunion in Clyde in June 1911. The 72nd O.V.I. was organized in nearby Fremont, Ohio, in October 1861 and included approximately 900 men from Erie, Medina, Sandusky, Seneca, Wood, and Ottawa Counties. They participated in numerous battles, campaigns, and administration for the Union army, including the Battle of Shiloh and the Siege of Vicksburg. Col. Ralph Buckland (1812–1892), of Fremont, commanded the unit. In all, the 72nd lost 298 men during the war—60 from combat and 238 from illness and disease. (Both, Randy Dick.)

Edward Payson Weston (1839–1929), labeled "II" in the image, strolled through Clyde on April 12, 1910. Weston, a Rhode Island native, was known as the "Father of Modern Pedestrianism" and frequently walked long distances across the country. In 1861, his first walk took him from Boston to Washington, DC—a distance of 478 miles—and took 10 days. Weston likely first walked through Clyde in 1867 during a trip from Portland, Maine, to Chicago. He repeated that walk in 1907, winding through Cleveland, Elyria, Oberlin, and Norwalk, Ohio, at an average pace of two miles per hour before spending the night in Clyde. The *Lewiston Evening Journal*, of Lewiston, Maine, reported that he "walked into Clyde, tired and sore, having completed a poor day's walk in his effort to beat his record of 40 years ago." Weston continued walking throughout his life. As cars became popular in the early 20th century, Weston warned that they made people lazy and sedentary. He died in 1929, two years after being struck by a taxi, which left him unable to walk. (John Sanford.)

# Two

# A Great Place to Live

This section of West Buckeye Street, now the site of Clyde's post office and the First Financial Bank, once contained a row of stately Victorian homes. From the left in this 1911 image, the first home was owned by Dave Heffner, a prominent lawyer; the First Financial parking lot is now on this site. The First Financial Bank is now located on the sites of the second and third homes. The second home belonged to G.P. Huntley, a jeweler, and the third home was built by local grocer Fred Curtis. The post office is now located on the site of the fourth and fifth homes. Dr. J.F. Whittemore, known for his dinner parties, owned the fourth home, while Harry Crockett owned the fifth home. Both properties were purchased by the federal government in 1937 to facilitate construction of the new post office. East Buckeye Street is visible in the distance. (Randy Dick.)

This undated postcard view of West Buckeye Street showcases the homes and tall trees that lined the street, much as they still do today. Note the brick road surface. Longtime Clyde residents may remember when Buckeye Street and adjacent George Street were paved with brick rather than asphalt. (John Sanford.)

Trees line West Buckeye Street in this postcard view looking west from the intersection with George Street. The scene presented here is not dramatically different from the how this scene would look today. The Clyde Public Library is visible at left, and homes line the opposite side of the street. Note the labeling street sign and the horse-pulled wagon. (John Sanford.)

This view of West Buckeye Street, looking east, offers a glimpse at homes along the south side of the street during the early 20th century. The scene looks very similar today. Main Street is visible in the far distance, while the Methodist church, Clyde Public Library, and the building that is now the Buckeye Rest Home are more clearly visible. In addition to the brick street, note the fire hydrant in the foreground. (Randy Dick.)

A close-up view of the home at 234 West Buckeye Street provides a look at the prominent chimneys incorporated into the architecture. This home is now the Buckeye Rest Home, but was formerly the Colvin Nursing Home. The home was renovated by local architect Thaddeus Hurd, with an addition completed in 1957. (John Sanford.)

This home at 235 West Buckeye Street is still standing and looks much the same today as it does in this 1906 holiday postcard. It was built in 1891. The windows are striking features, including the three rectangular windows on the side, two round windows in the upstairs, and one half-moon window on the side. The home remains a private residence. (Paula Renfro.)

This view of West Buckeye Street provides a glimpse of the stately homes along the north side of the street during the early 20th century. Many of these homes are still there today. The view is looking east, so Main Street is visible in the distance. A combination of horse-drawn wagons and automobiles appear to be traveling the brick street together. (John Sanford.)

A group of unidentified people stand on the front porch of the home of Dr. James and Ella Ott at 133 West Buckeye Street. The home is no longer standing but would have been located between where the post office and bank stand along that block today. (Lynn Monday.)

Clyde residents and Buckeye Street neighbors stand along Buckeye Street following a snowstorm in 1913. They are, from left to right, Winfield Adair, Joe Hunt, Dr. James Ott, and Frank Letson. (Clyde Museum.)

Two postcard views of Buckeye Street during the Great Flood of 1913 show the severity of the damage Clyde and the surrounding region experienced during that disaster. The Great Flood of 1913 remains the largest weather disaster ever recorded in Ohio. It rained from Easter Sunday, March 23, 1913, until March 27. The total recorded rainfall topped eight inches in some areas. Before the rain arrived, hurricane-force winds swept the region on Good Friday, March 21, 1913. Gusts of 100 miles per hour were recorded in nearby Toledo, Ohio. The wind shattered windows, broke utility poles, and snapped utility lines. Across the state, 428 people were killed, including three people in nearby Fremont and nineteen people in nearby Tiffin. (Both, Clyde Museum.)

This view of West Forest Street looks east toward Main Street from Buckeye Street and shows an unpaved road lined with homes and the wood-frame Lutheran church, which existed prior to the current stone church, on the corner. In 1912, the *Clyde Enterprise* reported that bricklaying was in progress on the street, which would make it "one of the finest in town when finished." (Randy Dick.)

This Shingle Style home once stood on West Forest Street next to the wood-frame Lutheran church. It served as the parsonage for the church for many years. It was most likely torn down with the frame church to make room for the new, current stone church, which was dedicated in 1928. (John Sanford.)

East Forest street is shown here in a view looking from Main Street following a snowstorm on February 14, 1909. Homes and trees line the street, and a streetlight hangs from a cable. (Clyde Museum.)

West Cherry Street in Clyde is shown on Christmas Day in 1906 in this photograph postcard. The view looks east toward the intersection of Cherry and George Streets. (Clyde Museum.)

Two young children play in front of a home in Clyde as two women look on from the porch. The postcard is undated but might be from the late 19th or early 20th century. Note that one child is riding a rocking horse, and the home includes modest Gothic details. (John Sanford.)

This 1906 postcard includes a note from Alice Kidman to a friend and shows the farmhouse she owned with her husband, James Kidman, outside of Clyde on North Ridge Road. Sunnyside, also known at that time as the "old Wilcox farm," sat on approximately 100 acres of land. Alice, a widow with one daughter, Mabel, married James Kidman in 1896. They had four more children, Ruth, James, Walter, and Sarah. Alice Kidman died in 1928 and is buried in McPherson Cemetery. (Paula Renfro.)

An unidentified family poses for a photograph outside their home in Clyde in this postcard. Note the child in the baby carriage among the family and the wooden swing in the yard. (Clyde Museum.)

Two children play in front of this home in Clyde as a woman, perhaps their mother, looks on. The postcard photograph is undated, but based on the clothing that people—particularly the children—are wearing, it is most likely from the very early 20th century. The boy appears to be holding a fishing pole. (Randy Dick.)

Lifelong Clyde resident Stella (Miller) Russell was born in 1891. She is shown here at her home in 1910 at age 19. She graduated from Clyde High School in 1909, married Charles Russell in 1916, and had three sons. She died in 1989. Toward the end of her life, she was viewed—at least by local reporters at the *Clyde Enterprise*—as a source of memory to confirm information about Clyde, such as where certain homes or businesses were once located. This postcard is a holiday card that Russell made for her friend Hazel Harvey. The details of everyday life in Clyde in this image are striking; note the framed beach scene on the wall, the wallpaper, and Russell's shoes. (Randy Dick.)

Longtime Clyde resident Lois Smila Hall (1903–2003), is shown in this 1903 photograph postcard at four months old. Hall was born in McComb, Ohio, and moved with her parents to Clyde in 1906. She graduated from Clyde High School in 1921, then married Frank C. Hall, who owned and operated a photography studio in Clyde. (Clyde Museum.)

Lois Smila Hall, on the left in this postcard photograph, is shown at age 10 in front of her family's home in Clyde, with a friend. The postcard is dated August 1, 1913. (Clyde Museum.)

An unidentified woman stands on the front porch of a home in Clyde in this early-20th-century postcard. While details about this particular scene are unknown, it provides a window into the everyday life of Clyde residents during this time. (Paula Renfro.)

A group of men at work on a farm in Clyde takes a break to pose for this photograph with children in April 1910. One man in the photograph is wearing work clothes and holding a paint can, and the boy is standing on a pile of boards and holding a saw. Part of a wooden frame bisects the corner of the photograph. (Clyde Museum.)

Two 20th-century postcard views of farms located outside of downtown Clyde offer windows into rural life during the first half of the century. In the above postcard, the Stokes family farm, located outside of downtown Clyde in Riley Township, is shown in the distance. John Stokes was born at the farm in 1851 and became one of the area's most well-known farmers and horticulturalists; he died in 1915. The below postcard provides a closer view of another expansive farm in Clyde in February 1934. Note the utility poles. The pole in the foreground features a sign pointing toward Toledo, Ohio, along with some advertisements. (Both, Clyde Museum.)

In 1897, the *Clyde Enterprise* reported that residents of Amanda Street, shown here on both postcards, asked the city to "pave the street to a width of 24 or 25 feet using paving brick laid in sand and cement," making it "the finest resident street in town." A 1915 poem, "On Amanda Street," compares it to other area streets and boasts, "I've heard folks brag about Big Bug Street, / And some think Cherry is hard to beat; / That Forest is pretty, and State is wide, / But to me the best old street in Clyde / Is Amanda street." (Above, Randy Dick; below, Clyde Museum.)

Amanda Street looks impassible after a snowstorm in November 1913. The storm damaged trees and utility lines and poles all across town, especially outside of the city. The *Clyde Enterprise* reported that "many of the north and south country roads will be impassable for days." (Randy Dick.)

An unidentified resident of Clyde poses for the photograph on this early-20th-century postcard. The photograph was taken by Frank C. Hall, who owned Hall's Photograph Studio in Clyde. (Clyde Museum.)

This house at 115 Duane Street was the home of local veterinarian Carl M. Prentice (1890–1945.) The Prentice family included Carl; his wife, Ethel; and their two children, Harold and Pauline. Dr. Prentice established his veterinary practice near his home in Clyde in 1912. (Ohio History Connection.)

A young Harold Prentice (1916–1983) is shown in this undated postcard photograph. A lifelong resident of Clyde, he was the son of local veterinarian Carl M. Prentice and his wife, Ethel. Harold graduated from Clyde High School in 1935 and later served in World War II. He married his wife, Francis, in 1945, and they had three children—Carl, Trudi, and Carol. Harold worked at Whirlpool in Clyde until his retirement in 1983. He is buried in McPherson Cemetery. (Ohio History Connection.)

A Busy Day on White Street.

In this photograph taken on September 2, 1910, a "building bee" is underway along White Street near the present-day intersection with Mulberry Street. It was organized by real estate developer Irving Jordan, who was constructing six homes. Jordan was a local businessman who made a living dealing in poultry and produce. Nearly a dozen teams of horses hauled gravel, hardware, plumbing supplies, lumber, and cement while visitors looked on. Note the workers standing on the porches of the homes and the scaffolding around the newest homes. The prices for the homes started at $2,000, and they contained "the best modern conveniences," according to the *Clyde Enterprise*. Jordan also graveled the road, poured cement sidewalks, and planted shade trees, "making a handsomest street of it." Jordan died in 1922 and is buried in McPherson Cemetery. This section of White Street still looks very similar today. (Randy Dick.)

# Three

# A GREAT PLACE TO WORK

M.L. Huss (d. 1931) and E. Van Benschoten (d. 1947), automobile dealers, are pictured in 1910 in this photograph postcard outside their dealership on West Buckeye Street, the Clyde Auto Sales Company, with a delivery of six Brush Runabouts. According to the *Clyde Enterprise*, all of the cars were sold before they shipped. "This firm has delivered 22 of these popular machines this season and cannot get nearly enough to supply the demand." The Brush Runabout was billed as "Everyman's car everyday" and retailed for $485. Van Benschoten, known locally as "Van," was one of the city's first automobile dealers. He sold the dealership in 1916 to another dealer in neighboring Fremont. Note the people around the cars and the signage on the dealership advertising "Garage," "Goodyear Tires," and "Brush Runabouts." (Randy Dick.)

The man in this postcard photograph is most likely Edward Geiger, who owned a local meat market. The cart behind the horse includes a box that might have been used to transport salted or cold meats. The lettering on the box reads "Geiger," and the business is listed in the 1913 Clyde city directory. (Clyde Museum.)

A group of 11 men works to repave Vine Street with bricks in this undated photograph postcard. Stacks of additional bricks are visible in the background. (Clyde Museum.)

The H.C. Kistler general store was located at 151 Washington Street, near the intersection with Vine Street, close to Clyde's interurban station. Clyde's 1913 city directory lists Homer Kistler as the proprietor, with his store selling fruits, candy, cigars, tobacco, ice cream, and groceries. Note the signs advertising Honest Scrap tobacco, Moxie cola, and Coca-Cola. (Randy Dick.)

Veterinarian Carl M. Prentice (1890–1945) is shown examining a dog inside the "dog room" at his office in Clyde. Prentice was a native of nearby Vickery, Ohio, and a graduate of Margaretta High School in nearby Castalia, Ohio. He graduated veterinary school at Ohio State University in 1912, the same year he married his wife, Ethel, and established his practice in Clyde. They had two children, Harold and Pauline. Carl, an avid hunter and sportsman, died during a hunting outing near Clyde in 1945. (Ohio History Connection.)

The Clyde Cooperage Company made barrels in Clyde from 1902 until 1914. Barrels were manufactured and sold locally or shipped by train and often used for making sauerkraut, bourbon, lard, and cider. The building was located along railroad tracks to facilitate supply delivery and shipments. Timber was shipped in from West Virginia, and finished barrels were shipped to fulfill orders. When it opened in 1902, the company employed 60 men and produced approximately 600 barrels a day. In 1913, the *Clyde Enterprise* reported that the company shipped 15 train cars of barrels each day, with each car holding 220 barrels, to locations in Ohio, Indiana, Kentucky, and Pennsylvania. In 1914, the Clyde Cooperage Company closed and moved to Toledo, Ohio. Joseph Walde (1877–1963) was the manager of the company; he was also the vice president of the Clyde Produce Company. (Randy Dick.)

This undated postcard advertises Mary E. French's astrology services. According to the 1908 city directory, French was married to Almon B. French, a local nursery owner. *Raphael's Ephemeris*, first published in 1824 by Robert Cross Smith (1795-1832), remains popular among astrologers; it is among the oldest of the zodiac ephemerides. (Paula Renfro.)

George Decker waits for a mail train at the railroad depot in Clyde in this undated photograph postcard. He carted the mail from the train to the post office, which was then located on Main Street. (Clyde Museum.)

The Hunter Tool Company manufactured a variety of hand tools in Clyde, including pruning shears and socket wrenches. The Hunter brothers opened a blacksmith shop in 1869 that grew into the tool company. This advertising postcard is undated, but records indicate that the company was sold in 1892. (Randy Dick.)

The notation on the back of this postcard reads: "Mother and Willy Myers at Myers' grocery store, Clyde, Ohio. Mother worked in the store." The photograph is undated. (Lynn Monday.)

Ess's Restaurant opened in 1925 at 117 East McPherson Highway. It is shown in this 1950s photograph postcard. The restaurant was listed among the finest eating places in the country in the Duncan Hines company's annual publication *Adventures in Good Eating*, which began in 1936 as a published compilation of places where Duncan Hines dined during his travels. After the restaurant closed, the building housed a salon, Carole Jean's Hair Fashion. (Randy Dick.)

Smith's Restaurant was located along McPherson Highway at the intersection with East Street. The postcard view shows a sign advertising "Home cooked and balanced meals" for 40¢. The postcard is undated, but is likely from the 1930s or 1940s. Note the "Linco" fuel pumps in front of the restaurant. (Lynn Monday.)

The Hughes Granite Company was once located at 111–127 East Buckeye Street in Clyde. The company made tombstones, monuments, markers, memorials, and mausoleums for customers across the country. Carmi Sanford (d. 1894) started the company in approximately 1884. He was very active in the community, including serving as one of the first officers of the People's Bank. He died in 1894 and is buried in McPherson Cemetery. After Sanford's death, his business partner and brother-in-law, William Hughes, managed the company's operations. Hughes was born in Clyde in 1862 and was a graduate of Clyde High School and the Spencerian School in Cleveland. He incorporated the Hughes Granite Company in 1894 and managed it until his death in 1921. By the time he died, Hughes had acquired quarry interests in Vermont and organized the American Mausoleum Company. The national trade journal *Monumental News* estimated that Hughes oversaw the building of over 100 mausoleums across the country during his career. The Hughes Granite Company building was later home to the Clyde Tool and Dye Works, the Clyde Auto Parts Company, and Dining Insurance and Accounting. The building was demolished in 1975. (Randy Dick.)

The Hughes Granite Company became nationally known for its work. The company beat 11 other firms in a design contest to create 35 monuments for Ohio's Battlefield Commission at what would become Shiloh National Military Park in Tennessee. In addition to creating the monuments, the company agreed to deliver them to the park. The 16-ton monuments were shipped by train, then transported by barge down the Tennessee River to Pittsburg Landing, where they were hoisted up the 100-foot bluff to the battlefield. The monuments were dedicated in 1902. The above photograph shows the company's modeling room and showroom. The below photograph shows the company's cutting room. (Both, Rutherford B. Hayes Presidential Library and Museums.)

These two views of the Clyde Kraut Company, located at 106–114 Church Street, provide a wide look at the once booming sauerkraut production industry in Clyde. The Clyde Kraut Company was established in 1890 and helped to put Clyde on the national map for sauerkraut production. "Judging by the number of cabbage wagons on the street, one would imagine that cabbage is coming to Clyde from the four corners of the earth," speculated the *Clyde Enterprise* in 1896. In these postcards, the company's proximity to railroad tracks, as well as at least one home, is visible. The Clyde Kraut Company continued production well into the 20th century. The factory was destroyed by a fire in 1968. (Above, Randy Dick; below, John Sanford.)

Two postcard views of cabbage deliveries to the "Comstock and Slessman's Kraut Factory" (aka the Clyde Kraut Company) in October 1906 show how the factory received its cabbage and how local farmers contributed to the company's success. In the above postcard, Clyde farmer George Streeter (1872–1952) delivers a load of cabbage. The sign on Streeter's wagon proclaims, "Banner load of the season, net weight 16,000 pounds," while Streeter's notes on the postcard state that "A load weighing 18,000 [pounds] came in after this." According to Basil Meek's *Twentieth Century History of Sandusky County, Ohio*, published in 1909, the members of the Streeter family were among the "highly respected citizens of Green Creek Township" and owned 165 acres of land between Green Creek and nearby York Township. In the below postcard, two farmers arrive with a heaping wagonload of cabbage. The weight—16,800 pounds—is written in chalk on the side of the wagon. Signs for Silver Fleece Kraut, the Clyde Kraut Company's trademarked brand, and the factory office, are prominent. (Above, Randy Dick; below, Clyde Museum.)

This promotional postcard offers greetings from Clyde, the "Sauerkraut Town," with images of scenes from around the city. Clockwise from top left, the images show the James B. McPherson statue in McPherson Cemetery, Clyde Public Library, Waterworks Pond, the Baptist church, Clyde Kraut Company, the McPherson Cemetery entrance, and Main Street. (Randy Dick.)

This promotional postcard was published by Clyde resident M.D. Brown sometime in the early 20th century. This particular card was postmarked 1908. By 1909, the Clyde Kraut Company was the largest manufacturer of sauerkraut in the United States and employed over 100 men, processing 1,000 pounds of sauerkraut each day. In and around Clyde, an estimated 4,000 acres of farmland were devoted to growing cabbage for the annual production of sauerkraut. (Randy Dick.)

Employees of the Clyde Kraut Company pose for a photograph outside of the factory in this undated postcard. The Silver Fleece Kraut brand sign is prominent. The employees were mostly men, although there were a few women. (Clyde Museum.)

This display at the Clyde Kraut Company contained enough canned sauerkraut for "2,000,000 meals," as noted on the sign. The production line of cans, with cans in production, is visible. Silver Fleece was the company's trademarked brand. In addition to sauerkraut, the company also pickled cucumbers and canned cherries. (Randy Dick.)

The Clyde Kraut Company also produced canned cherries under the Silver Fleece brand. This postcard shows what was probably a parade float for the company featuring a "bowl full of cherries." In July 1942, the *Clyde Enterprise* reported that the Clyde Kraut Company's cherry "pick" for the season topped out at 800 tons. Of the final supply, 44 percent was earmarked for the military for distribution to soldiers during World War II. (John Sanford.)

The Clyde Produce Company, a sauerkraut production facility located on East Buckeye Street, was managed by Henry Parker, a lifelong resident of Clyde who was born in 1866. The Clyde Produce Company manufactured Pride of Clyde sauerkraut. Parker owned a cider mill, which he sold to the Clyde Kraut Company in exchange for shares of stock in that company. In approximately 1906, he sold his interest in the Clyde Kraut Company and bought the Clyde Produce Company from O.M. Mallernee. In 1909, the company employed 35 men and processed enough cabbage to fill 150 train cars. (Paula Renfro.)

The Elmore Manufacturing Company was located at 504 Amanda Street. The business was started by Harmon Von Vechten Becker and his sons, James and Burton, in nearby Elmore, Ohio, in 1892, and initially manufactured bicycles. The company began making cars in 1893. In 1909, General Motors bought Elmore Manufacturing. Production continued in Clyde until 1912, when the factory closed and the Elmore car brand was subsumed into General Motors production in Michigan. The Elmore manufacturing space later became the home of the Krebs Commercial Car Company (1912–1917) and the successful Clydesdale Motor Truck Company (1917–1939). The factory complex later became a part of Clyde Porcelain and Steel known as "Plant 2." It was demolished in 1972. (Above, Randy Dick; below, Clyde Museum.)

The factory floor at the Elmore Manufacturing Company is shown from two different angles in these postcards. Both images depict quiet-looking scenes with few or no workers pictured. The Elmore Manufacturing workspace was open and had individual workstations for assembly—different from more modern assembly line setups. Note the equipment in each photograph, as well as the workspace details such as windows, lights, and beams in the ceiling. Employee timecards are arranged on the wall in the foreground at far right in the above image. The below photograph shows a pulley system in the factory ceiling, a worker hauling a pile of boxes with a pushcart, and what appear to be finished cars with sheets over them in the background. (Above, John Sanford; below, Randy Dick.)

Three Elmore car models gained popularity: the Elmore Convertible Runabout seated four passengers and sold for $650; the three-speed Elmore Runabout seated two passengers and sold for $800; and the top-of-the-line three-speed Elmore Tonneau seated four passengers and sold for $1,400. Elmore claimed to offer "the only double-cylinder motor in the world that [could] be started without cranking." The double-cylinder engine allowed the company to market the cars as "valveless," thus the company's slogan was "The Car That Has No Valves." (James Semon.)

The Elmore Manufacturing Company showroom, shown in 1908, featured all of the available vehicle models, including the famed Pathfinder. The trophy and sign on the floor are sitting in front of a race-winning Elmore "Bulldog." Note the sign in the background proclaiming the Elmore to be "the simplest car in the world" due to its "valveless" construction. (Clyde Museum.)

In 1908, an Elmore Pathfinder driven by Andy Smith, of Los Angeles, won the Cactus Derby, a 500-mile road race that went from Los Angeles, California, to Phoenix, Arizona. Dubbing his Elmore "The Bulldog," Smith finished the course in approximately 31 hours. The winning Pathfinder is shown here at the Elmore factory with the prize cup that Smith won. This was one of several races that included Elmore cars in the early 20th century. Another Elmore Pathfinder

won the American Automobile Association–sponsored race from New York to the St. Louis World's Fair in 1904; an Elmore car competed for the prized Glidden Cup in 1905 and 1906; and in 1909, on the Munsy Tour from Washington, DC, to Boston, the Elmore was the only car to go the entire distance with a perfect record. (Clyde Museum.)

The Krebs Commercial Car Company was established by J.C.L. "Louis" Krebs in 1912 and occupied the former Elmore Manufacturing Company space. Krebs employed approximately 50 former Elmore workers. Despite the "car company" name, the Krebs company manufactured small trucks. The *Clyde Enterprise* described the Krebs Commercial Car as a "neat, light, and compact vehicle for truck work." In 1917, the Krebs Commercial Car Company merged with two other companies to create the Clydesdale Motor Truck Company. (James Semon.)

The Krebs Commercial Car was open, and the mechanisms that drove the truck are visible. The company eventually patented a multispeed engine governor that could control and maintain speed (similar to today's cruise control). When Krebs merged with two other companies to form the Clydesdale Motor Truck Company in 1917, the Krebs engine governor became a prominent feature on Clydesdale trucks and was marketed as the "Driver Under the Hood." (James Semon.)

The Clydesdale Motor Truck Company was located on Amanda Street in the former Elmore Car Company factory space. The company was incorporated in 1917 and manufactured truck chassis. Most of the company's early inventory was shipped overseas for use during World War I. The Clydesdale Company was at the forefront of truck manufacturing during the early 20th century, when trucks were relatively new in the automobile industry, and catered to a global market after the war. The Clydesdale Motor Truck Company enjoyed a prosperous couple of decades but dissolved in 1939 during the Great Depression. (James Semon.)

A row of Clydesdale truck chassis sit outside the factory. Customers could purchase a chassis directly from the factory, then contract with a third-party truck-body builder to develop a custom truck. As a result of this production and sales model, Clydesdale trucks functioned in an array of industries for a variety of customers—garbage trucks, delivery trucks, farm trucks, tanker trucks, fire trucks, and even railroad maintenance equipment with track-compatible wheels, for example. All Clydesdale trucks featured the company's patented "Driver Under the Hood," a multispeed engine governor that functioned in way similar to that of modern cruise control technology. (James Semon.)

G.S. Pickett stands among cherry trees that were part of the Clyde Nursery and Greenhouses. He bought the nursery in 1881 from Almon B. French, who had established it in 1863. It was located along McPherson Highway and was among the largest in the state at that time. (Lynn Monday.)

An 1898 business postcard for the French Nursery highlights the variety of plants that the nursery offered. Almon B. French was born in Trumbull County, Ohio, in 1838, and moved to Clyde in 1859. In addition to opening his nursery, French gained fame as a public medium. He also eventually studied law and passed the Ohio bar exam. French was nominated to serve as a state representative in 1898 but declined the offer. He died in 1923 and was buried in McPherson Cemetery. (John Sanford.)

### ESTABLISHED IN 1863.
## G. S. PICKETT & SON,
### PROPRIETORS OF THE

### GREEN HOUSES.

A General Assortment of Fruit and Ornamental Trees, Grape Roots, Hedge Plants, Flowering Shrubs, Green House and Bedding Plants, Cut Flowers, Boquets, &c.

## ORDERS PROMPTLY FILLED.
### CLYDE, OHIO.
(OVER)

This business postcard for G.S. Pickett's Clyde Nursery and Greenhouses dates to 1888 and promises "orders promptly filled." It also showcases the extensive variety of plants available at the nursery. (John Sanford.)

### 250 Acres Devoted to Nursery and Orchards

ESTABLISHED 1863

## THE CLYDE NURSERY

A. R. Pickett & Son, Proprs.

### CLYDE, OHIO

Fruit and Ornamental Trees, Shrubs, Roses, Grape Vines, Berries, etc.

Represented by

_____

In 1921, G.S. Pickett's son, A.R. Pickett, and his grandsons Royce, Harold, and Robert Pickett expanded the nursery business to 250 acres and shortened the name to the Clyde Nursery. The Picketts remained fixtures in the local fruit and orchard market well into the 20th century. (Randy Dick.)

The Clyde Cutlery Company was established in 1850 in nearby Norwalk, Ohio. In 1892, owner Samuel James and his sons, Laurence and Robert, bought the Hunter Tool Company and expanded operations to Clyde. The company was located off of Main Street along the railroad tracks on East Buckeye Street. Initially employing just 10 people, the company manufactured carving and butcher knives and pruning shears. The two views here show how the main building of the company was a three-story brick structure. A two-story addition was erected in 1919. The plant caught fire in 1970, and the company was unable to recover. At that time, it was Clyde's longest-running business. The building was leveled in 1972 to clear land for the new city hall. (Both, Clyde Museum.)

A display of Clyde Cutlery Company products appears to be ready for a parade in this undated photograph. Clyde Cutlery Company patented a "draw cut" pruning blade that was immensely popular. All of the knives were hand-forged and hand-tempered and came in a variety of sizes. The four-inch blade with a maple handle sold for 25¢. In 1902, the *Clyde Enterprise* reported that the company manufactured approximately 150 knives each day, as well as pruning shears, to meet high demand. Clyde Cutlery knives included an aluminum handle that was welded onto the knife blade in such a way that prevented dust and grease from accumulating. During World War I, the Clyde Cutlery Company produced machetes and military products. It later produced stainless steel spatulas and grill tools for home use in addition to knives. (Randy Dick.)

A 1940s promotional postcard for the Clyde Cutlery Company traces the company's history since 1850, and acknowledges its longtime presence in Clyde. The factory space is shown as it changed over time. The Clyde Cutlery Company closed following a devastating fire in 1970. (Clyde Museum.)

A barbershop in Clyde looks busy in this undated photograph as a barber tends to a customer. This barbershop was located inside the Nichols House hotel along Railroad Street. The architectural and decorative details of the shop are visible here. (Lynn Monday.)

The Universal Paper Products Company, shown in the above postcard, was established in Chicago in 1911 by three men—H.W. Bingham, president; E.L. Hamilton, secretary-treasurer; and J.C. Leach, vice president and manager. They opened the plant in Clyde in 1916, and it employed 200 workers. The factory was located along Amanda Street in an area that is now home to present-day Whirlpool facilities. In 1922, Bingham died, Hamilton retired, and the company was sold to Gardner & Harvey Company of Middletown, Ohio; its equipment was moved to Middletown. In 1923, the building became home to the Vitrified Iron Products Company, shown below. Vitrified Iron Products manufactured porcelain signs. One of the company's most remarkable signs was for the Lincoln Oil Refining Company (LINCO); it had letters that were nine feet tall and was installed on a tower on top of the Merchants National Bank Building in Indianapolis, Indiana. (Both, Randy Dick.)

The Davidson Enamel Company is shown here with the Vitrified Iron Products building in the background. The Davidson Enamel Company began production in Clyde in 1934 and manufactured a variety of porcelain and steel products, including porcelain bathroom tiles. In 1943, the company changed its name to Clyde Porcelain Steel. During World War II, Clyde Porcelain Steel manufactured military equipment, including doors for tanks. A fire reduced the factory to ashes in 1945. The blaze remains the largest single fire loss in Clyde history. In the days following the fire, employees arrived with rakes and shovels to assist in the cleanup and rebuilding, and the factory eventually reopened. The Whirlpool Corporation bought Clyde Porcelain Steel in 1952. Today, the Whirlpool facility is Clyde's largest employer and among the largest washing machine–producing operations in North America. (Clyde Museum.)

# Four

# A GREAT PLACE TO VISIT

The Nichols House, a three-story hotel, was located on Railroad Street opposite the railroad depot. The redbrick building with wrought iron balconies was built in 1867 by Henry Nichols and was advertised in the first issue of the *Clyde Enterprise* when it began production in 1878. Nichols died in 1882, but the hotel remained open, changing owners over time. The hotel was known for its dining room and often hosted entertainers who were performing at the Clyde Opera House, which was on Main Street. In 1907, A.B. Davenport and his son-in-law, E.A. Meeker, bought the hotel. Davenport was a longtime hotel manager who was "favorably known to the traveling public," according to the *Enterprise*. Meeker was chief engineer on the Great Lakes steamer *I.W. Nicholas* and worked at the hotel seasonally. Davenport and Meeker wrote in the *Enterprise*, "A first class [hotel] in a community is not to be underestimated. It is an important factor, in quite the same category as good waterworks, good churches, good schools, and good newspapers." The Nichols House closed sometime after 1921. (Randy Dick.)

In addition to the Nichols House, Clyde was home to a second downtown hotel located at 118 West Maple Street. The hotel opened as the Empire House in 1886 and was operated by Frank Welker, who was born in Hancock County, Ohio, in 1849 and moved to Clyde in 1864. He was known as a "genial and popular proprietor." Prior to opening the hotel, Welker had been a brakeman on the Lake Shore & Michigan Southern Railroad. The hotel operated on "the European plan." Rooms could be rented by the day or week, and the dining room would serve everything on its menu for the season from 6:00 a.m. until 8:00 p.m. Welker died in 1908 and was buried in McPherson Cemetery. The same year, Empire House was sold to the Long family, of Mansfield, Ohio, and renamed the Clyde Hotel. In 1911, the hotel was sold to C.A. Ward, who also bought the Nichols House. The Clyde Hotel later became Ye Wayside Inne. The Empire House features prominently in Sherwood Anderson's *Winesburg, Ohio* as the New Willard House. (Above, John Sanford; below, Randy Dick.)

The railroad depot in Clyde was located on Railroad Street, just off Main Street, near the intersection of two rail lines that ran through the city and not far from the downtown hotels. It was built in 1876 in a Gothic Revival style and replaced a smaller depot structure at the same site. The first railroads were built in Clyde in 1852. Two rail lines intersected in Clyde: the Lake Shore & Michigan Southern Railroad ran east-west; and the Cleveland, Cincinnati, Chicago, & St. Louis Railroad, or the "Big Four" line, ran north-south. Both lines were part of the New York Central Railroad. In the era before automobiles, the train offered basic transportation for residents throughout the region. According to the city directory from 1887, trains stopped at the depot in Clyde 18 times each day for passengers and twice for freight. Residents could take trains to and from nearby Sandusky, Toledo, or Cleveland for daytime or overnight trips. The depot stood in the southeast angle of the intersection of the two lines and was L-shaped to serve both lines. The depot was demolished in the summer of 1960. (Above, Randy Dick; below, Clyde Museum.)

Starting in 1832, regular stagecoach service began in Clyde. Schedules were printed in the 1887 city directory and showed several departures and arrivals each day. In this 19th-century postcard, a driver appears to be ferrying visitors, most likely to a local hotel. (Clyde Museum.)

This postcard shows an express stagecoach service stopped in Clyde on October 12, 1910. The name "Express Coach" is visible above the front window of the wagon. A sign for "Livery" is visible in the background. (Paula Renfro.)

The interurban station in Clyde offered another mode of transportation to people in Clyde in the early 20th century. It provided service to Cleveland, Toledo, and points between in either direction via the Lake Shore Electric Railway. Service started in 1901 and continued until 1939, offering passengers "speedy service" to nearby locations including Norwalk, Sandusky, Milan, Huron, Vermilion, Lorain, Elyria, Bellevue, Fremont, Gibsonburg, and Genoa. It took approximately four hours to travel the entire line from Cleveland to Toledo. Clyde's interurban station was located next to Kistler's grocery store near the present-day intersection of Vine Street and McPherson Highway, which is labeled "State Street" on this postcard. Note the horse-drawn carriage parked outside the station, the people on the sidewalk in the distance, and the people sitting in the station. (John Sanford.)

Comic travel postcards were common in the early 20th century, especially after 1907, when postcards could be printed with a divided back, leaving room for a message on the left and a mailing address on the right. Companies printed postcards like this with a variety of city names imprinted in the areas where "Clyde, Ohio" is displayed. Although these postcards are not unique to Clyde, they showcase an example of travel, mailing, and marketing history. (Both, Randy Dick.)

Postcards like these were inexpensive, widely available, and easy to send to friends and loved ones. The comic messages printed on the cards were often humorous or pithy statements. In these examples, there are references to train travel, car trips, and even immigration. (Both, Randy Dick.)

Another example of a promotional postcard from the early 20th century offers "glimpses of Clyde." It features photographs of local scenes and buildings and was most likely produced by a local photographer who would have had access to these images. Pictured on the postcard are, clockwise from top left, the Methodist Episcopal church, Clyde Baptist Church, the railroad depot, Union School, and a scene from Main Street. (John Sanford.)

This photograph postcard of two men standing behind a car cutout was sent from a long-term visitor to Clyde to his sister in Toledo in February 1912. The photograph was most likely staged in a photography studio. The Clyde city directories from 1909 and 1913 list Elliott's Photographic Studio at 112 East Buckeye Street as a local photographer. (Randy Dick.)

Clyde had a bus terminal located at the corner of Hamer Street and McPherson Highway. In addition to being a bus station, it was also a general store and had a lunch counter. Above, the station is shown with a Lake Shore Coach bus, which traveled between Clyde and Sandusky, Ohio. The bus terminal in Clyde was also a Greyhound bus stop. Later, the store and café were known as Bechler's General Store and, even later, Seaman's Pharmacy. (Both, Randy Dick.)

The Camp Grand Motel, or "tourist camp," was located along West McPherson Highway near Parkway Avenue. It was opened in 1928 by Lynn A. Harris and consisted of 32 buildings, including 29 cottages that could be rented like hotel rooms. According to the *Clyde Enterprise*, the "tourist camp idea" developed from a campground that once existed in Clyde and was operated by the Clyde Exchange Club. It offered accommodations for travelers who pitched their tents and cooked with campfires. Camp Grand featured a restaurant in the main building as well as a community kitchen for guests who stayed in the cabins. Recreational facilities included a miniature golf course, playground, horseshoe court, tennis courts, and a cactus garden. There was also a gas station on the northeast corner of the property. The camp soon became a stop along three bus routes that went through Clyde. It hosted reunions of local Civil War veterans in 1939 and 1941. Camp Grand was later owned by Lee Myers. It closed in 1958. (Both, Randy Dick.)

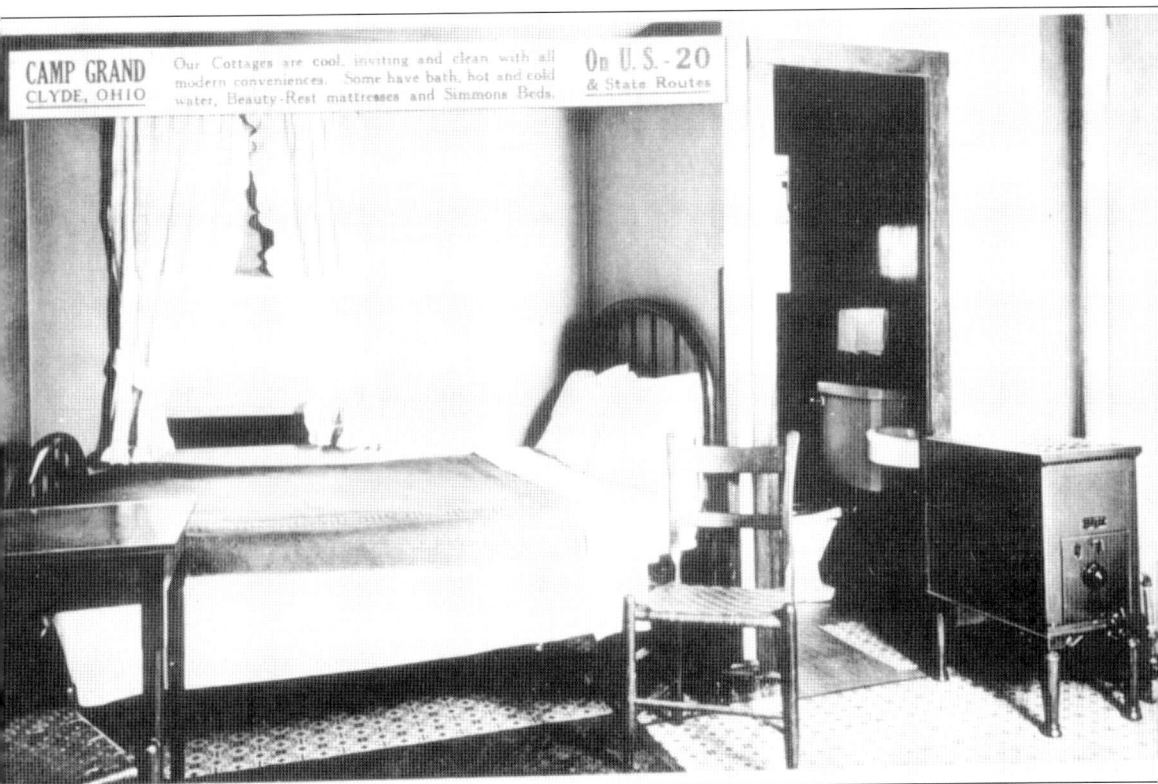

The cottages at Camp Grand were designed to be state-of-the-art for their time. They measured between 12-by-14 feet and 20-by-21 feet in size. Each cottage contained a private bathroom, electric lights, gas heating, a full-size bed, and a small table. Each cottage was slightly different in detail, and all of the wiring for the camp was underground, so there were no utility poles aboveground. When the camp opened in 1928, the *Clyde Enterprise* suggested that those who stayed at the camp "will be among those who are pleasure bent" and seeking "a certain novelty about a high class tourist camp." (Randy Dick.)

The Clyde Tourist Camp was another cottage rental facility, similar to Camp Grand, along McPherson Highway. It was built in the 1940s by Ben Street and later operated by Bill and Sue McMurtry. This camp was smaller than Camp Grand and offered 15 cabins and 23 cottages for rent. In the above postcard, the "Cabins" office is visible. Note the fuel pumps in front of the building. The "Cottages" building shown below is also visible above in the background at right. The below postcard provides a closer look at the "Cottages" building. There appear to be numerous swings and benches and other garden ornaments outside the cabins for guests to use or buy. (Above, John Sanford; below, Clyde Museum.)

The cottages at the Clyde Tourist Camp featured private baths and 24-hour service, according to this advertising postcard. Note the perspective of the photograph. There appears to be a man sitting to the right of the photographer. This view provides a closer look at the numerous swings and benches available to guests. A guest is sitting on a pony in the distance. (Paula Renfro.)

The Clyde Tourist Camp also featured an outdoor market where visitors or guests could purchase locally crafted products. The market is featured on this undated photograph postcard. A variety of wood, ceramic, metal, and pottery crafts are on display. (Randy Dick.)

The Bar-Zee Motel was located at 513 West McPherson Highway. It was one of several motels along McPherson Highway that operated throughout the 20th century. Perhaps one most interesting feature of the motel was its distinctive sign. There was also a swimming pool on the property for guests to enjoy. The Bar-Zee Motel was operated by Robert Zanger. (Both, Randy Dick.)

The Saddle Inn Motel was located at 214 East McPherson Highway near the corner of Maple Street and McPherson Highway. It has most recently been known as the Winesburg Inn. (Randy Dick.)

The Plaza Motel was located at 500 East McPherson Highway near the corner of East Street and McPherson Highway and across from McPherson Cemetery. (Randy Dick.)

This split postcard from 1964 shows the Ranger Motel and Bechler's General Store, which were located along McPherson Highway near the intersection with Hamer Street. The Ranger Motel was operated by John and Julia Tokas and advertised in-room telephones, individually controlled heat, ceramic-tile baths, air-conditioning, and connecting rooms. (John Sanford.)

A display along McPherson Highway (US Route 20) greets travelers as they enter Clyde. Similar signage is still in place around the city today. The display notes Clyde as the home of Sherwood Anderson's *Winesburg, Ohio* and as a Tree City USA community. The Tree City USA program is sponsored by the Arbor Day Foundation and recognizes cities that demonstrate a commitment to maintaining and expanding their tree or forest stock. Clyde was named a Tree City USA in 1983. (Randy Dick.)

# Five

# ALL AROUND THE TOWN

Union School, located on Vine Street, was built in 1870. It was not the first school built in Clyde; a series of log cabin schools around Hamer's Corners, near the present-day entrance to McPherson Cemetery, were the first, followed by a series of frame schools in Clyde's downtown. Union School was built at a cost of $40,000 and featured Italianate details, including a belfry. A one-story addition in the back of the building contained bathrooms and a boiler for steam heat. When the school opened in 1870, it housed all twelve grades: the first four grades were on the first floor, grades five through eight were on the second floor, and grades nine through twelve were on the third floor. F.M. Ginn was the superintendent in 1870. In 1875, the first class graduated from the school. It consisted of four students—one boy and three girls. Union School was torn down in 1937 after the Clyde High School (later the Clyde Junior High School) was built nearby on Spring Street. (Randy Dick.)

The third-grade class of the 1908–1909 school year stands in front of Union School in this postcard photograph. The photograph provides a close-up view of the front of the school, as well as of the diverse students who attended during that time and their teachers. (Randy Dick.)

The seventh-grade class of the 1908–1909 school year poses in front of Union School in this postcard photograph. Pictured here are, from left to right, (first row) James Mason, Sara Walden, ? Kette, ? Van Benschoten, and Carl Ringle; (second row) ? Bruggerman, George Bradford, Carrol Perin, Marie Krebs, Laurence Wolger, Sara R. Walden, ? McCleary, Bessie Weiker, and two unidentified; (third row) Joe Sloan, Laurence Friedley, Gladden Pickett, Irma Brown, Leola Hurd, Lawrence Carr, Clarence Fuller, and unidentified; (fourth row) Leon Greenslade, Ethel St. John, Rena Colvin, Lillian Wolger, Elsie Mears, and a Miss Quinlan. (Randy Dick.)

The building that would later be known as Vine Street School, an elementary school housing kindergarten through fourth grade, is shown in the above postcard, while Clyde Junior High School is shown below. Vine Street School opened at 521 Vine Street as Clyde High School in 1923. The building featured columns at the outside front entrance and marble staircases and hardwood and terrazzo floors inside. Walker and Norwich of Dayton, Ohio, were the architects, and the Hossler Brothers, of Tiffin, Ohio, were the contractors. The school featured large "domestic science," "manual training," and "agricultural" departments. The 1923 graduating class consisted of 28 students. Clyde Junior High School (later McPherson Middle School) was built around the corner from the high school, at 201 Spring Street, in 1937. It opened as Clyde High School, replacing the 1923 school, which was converted to an elementary school. Both schools closed in 2010 and were demolished in 2011. (Above, Randy Dick; below, Clyde Museum.)

The 1914–1915 Clyde High School boys basketball team is shown on this photograph postcard. Clyde High School basketball games were often played at Terry's Hall, formerly the Clyde Opera House, located on the second floor at 114 South Main Street. Admission to games was 25¢ for adults and 10¢ for children under 12. (Randy Dick.)

The 1919–1920 Clyde High School girls' basketball team is shown here. The players pictured are, from left to right, (front row) Jessie Purcell and Grace Slessman; (second row) Mildred Sutch, Anna Werth, and Heloise Killinger; (third row) Evelyn France Richards, Veta McCray, and Kay Brown. (Clyde Museum.)

This undated postcard shows a track meet that took place at the fairgrounds in Clyde with a track team from nearby Sandusky, Ohio. The expansive field and wooden grandstand are visible in the photograph, just as Sherwood Anderson describes the location in *Winesburg, Ohio*. The site of the fairgrounds, which included a racetrack, is now part of the land occupied by Clyde Elementary School. (John Sanford.)

Waterworks Pond, which is now part of Clyde Community Park, is shown in this c. 1910 postcard. A gazebo is shown in front of the waterworks facility, which boasted three prominent chimneys. Clyde's waterworks facility opened in 1883 following city approval of a $20,000 bond to fund the building of the pump house and development of the west reservoir (at left). The east reservoir (at right) was added in 1886. By 1887, the city boasted over three miles of pipe under the streets and 38 fire hydrants. (Clyde Museum.)

An unidentified man stands in front of a trailer of trunks in this undated photograph taken near downtown Clyde. Note the railroad tracks in the photograph, as well as the brick street surface. (John Sanford.)

This postcard shows hail that fell during a storm on June 3, 1891. The storm made news in California, as the *Sacramento Daily Union* reported a "vast amount of damage in Ohio and Indiana," and that at Clyde, "a storm of terrific hailstorms broke windows and door panels in houses and stores. Fifteen windows in a passenger car on the Wheeling and Lake Erie (rail)road were broken, the headlight smashed and a hole knocked in the roof of the cab." (Clyde Museum.)

The Merry Widows baseball team poses for the photograph featured on this early-20th-century postcard. Written on the back of the postcard is "Piety Hill Against the World." Piety Hill was located at the end of Race Street, near the city waterworks, and down the street from present-day Clyde Community Park. Frank C. Hall, who later operated a photography studio in Clyde, is pictured at far left in the second row. (Clyde Museum.)

In this undated postcard, the Camp Fire Girls of Clyde display a service flag that they presented to the city. A notation on the back of the postcard identifies the chief guardian of the Camp Fire group as "Sadie" and counts 225 stars on the flag. (Randy Dick.)

The Clyde Public Library opened in 1906 at the corner of West Buckeye and George Streets. Prior to the building of the library, local resident Rowena Baker maintained a reading room on West Buckeye Street in partnership with the Women's Christian Temperance Union. In 1903, a public library was established on the third floor of Union School, but it quickly outgrew its space. In 1904, Clyde resident Judge S.S. Richards wrote to industrialist and philanthropist Andrew Carnegie and asked for funding for a new building. Carnegie offered a $10,000 grant, which the citizens of Clyde matched. Leon Woodorth was the builder. The building featured glacial boulders split in two with the faces turned out and a tiled roof. Area farmers brought stones to the construction site and were paid $1 per wagonload. Carnegie provided construction grants to 2,509 libraries between 1883 and 1929. In 1919, it was estimated that he had funded construction of over half of the libraries in the United States at that time. (Randy Dick.)

This view of the library from 1919 showcases additional architectural details and provides a glimpse, in the extreme left of the image, of the William Wilder house, which used to stand behind the library. It was torn down in the 1980s to make space for the current library parking lot. Wilder was an executive with the Clyde Kraut Company and president of the National Kraut Packers Association. The library quickly became an important community resource in the city. In the late 20th century, the library was renovated with an addition, constructed in the same style as the original building. The addition was completed in 1996. Other interesting features in the image include the woman walking on the sidewalk and the fire hydrant along the street. (John Sanford.)

The main reading area of the Clyde Public Library is shown in 1910, four years after the library was built and opened to the public. The reference desk is clearly visible, as are shelves of books available for checkout. This portion of the library is still in use as a reading area. (John Sanford.)

The Buckeye Club basketball team is shown here in front of Hughes Granite Works along Buckeye Street. The club's official address was 107 East Buckeye Street. The photograph was taken by the Elliott Studio, and notes identify Lex Pawsey sitting next to the driver and Karl Hutchinson behind him (to the left in the photograph). (Clyde Museum.)

The Clyde Baseball Club was organized by Herman Hurd in 1894, and his friend, Sherwood Anderson, then age 17, was part of the team, serving as an umpire. This photograph postcard is not dated, but is from sometime after 1895. The team was known as the Stars in 1894 but the name was changed to the Greys by 1895. That year, the team got new uniforms paid for by a local merchant. It played at Ames Field, which was located near today's Ames Street, then the east edge of the city, and competed against other area baseball clubs, including the Oak Harbor Swamp Angels. In his *Memoirs*, Anderson writes about a celebratory evening with his teammates following a game, describing his "happiness, the warm feeling I now have for these others out here with me at the edge of the wood." (John Sanford.)

This postcard shows two unidentified men sitting at a restaurant or bar in Clyde in October 1913. Note the ornate display of desserts and the tall glasses of drink. (Clyde Museum.)

The Harkness Theatre, later the Clyde Theater, was located on West Buckeye Street. The building was brick with medallions on the facade. In 1932, the theater was renovated, with the *Clyde Enterprise* calling it improved to the point of being "one of the finest [theaters] in Northwestern Ohio." Theater officials boasted that every seat in the theater was "set at just the right angle for perfect vision and comfort." The theater eventually closed and was demolished in 1971. (Paula Renfro.)

Presbyterian Church, Clyde, Ohio.

First Presbyterian Church, located at 113 West Forest Street, was built in 1869 and dedicated in 1870. The Presbyterian Church Society of Clyde was organized in 1867 with 36 members who congregated at a local Baptist meetinghouse. When the church was completed in 1870, it resembled a red one-room schoolhouse. In 1893, under the pastorship of George Wilson, the church was remodeled. Wings containing galleries were added, which doubled the sanctuary's seating capacity. New windows were installed, along with the tower that contained the pastor's study. In 1912, a pipe organ was purchased from Trinity Chapel in Toledo and replaced the portable organ. The church is featured in Sherwood Anderson's *Winesburg, Ohio*, with the character Rev. Curtis Hartman, who sat in his study in the tower and watched the schoolteacher, Kate Swift, who lived in the house next door. (Randy Dick.)

St. Mary's Catholic Church, located at the intersection of Vine and Spring Streets, was dedicated in 1890, and the house next to it was completed in 1892. The Catholic congregation in Clyde was first organized in 1853, with Mass held in members' homes and priests regularly visiting Clyde. In 1858, the congregation purchased land at the corner of Spring and Vine Streets and built a frame church and started a cemetery. In 1886, construction began on the brick church that still stands there today. According to the 1887 city directory, when the cornerstone was laid, a time capsule containing period newspapers and photographs was placed inside. The church was built in a classical Gothic style, and the tall spire is visible from many points around town. When the church was dedicated in 1890, there were approximately 70 Catholic families in Clyde. The congregation opened a parochial school in 1956, which closed in 2010. (Clyde Museum.)

The cemetery that surrounds St. Mary's Catholic Church was consecrated in 1860. The land for the cemetery and the church was purchased in 1860 by a priest from nearby Fremont, Ohio, who was serving the Clyde parish. Clyde's first resident priest was assigned in 1872 following years of service by priests from nearby Fremont and Bellevue. (Clyde Museum.)

Grace Episcopal Church, located at 124 West Buckeye Street, was built in 1886. The building follows an American Gothic style of construction. It was dedicated in 1889 to Henry Paden, a founder of the congregation, former mayor of Clyde, and former editor and publisher of the *Clyde Enterprise* who had died the previous year. The congregation eventually left the church, and the building came under local ownership. It is now home to the Clyde Museum, which opened in 1987. (John Sanford.)

The Methodist Episcopal church, located at the corner of West Buckeye and George Streets, was built in 1867. The first Methodist congregation in Clyde was organized in 1820 and consisted of six people. They met in a log house that belonged to Samuel McMillan and was located near the intersection of Race and Maple Streets. In 1963, the congregation built a new church at the corner of Race and Maple Streets, near its original meeting place, and named it First Methodist Church—today, First United Methodist Church. In order to build the new church, the congregation demolished a greenhouse that stood on the site. During demolition, it was discovered that the original McMillan cabin was still standing as part of the structure. The bell from this church was installed in the new church. Since the congregation left this building in 1963, it has been used by several local organizations over the years. (Randy Dick.)

The interior of the Methodist Episcopal church, shown here in 1922, featured a large pipe organ. This postcard view also provides a look at the church pews, lighting, wall coverings, and other architectural details. (Ohio History Connection.)

Harold Prentice (1916–1983) is shown here with his Sunday school class at the Methodist Episcopal church on May 21, 1920. The class had just planted a cherry tree in the church parsonage yard. The names of everyone in the photograph are listed on the back of the postcard, and, in addition to Harold, include Harold's sister, Pauline Prentice; Donald Killinger; Sammy Killinger; Mary Westerhouse; Awilda Keyse; Helene Hummel; Ralph Abbott; Iona Hall; Agnes Franks; Donald Carter; and Betty Hefner. (Ohio History Connection.)

This frame church stood at the corner of West Forest and George Streets and was the home of the Lutheran congregation in Clyde prior to the current structure in that location, St. Paul's Lutheran Church. It was the first church constructed in Clyde and was built by a Universalist congregation prior to the Civil War. The Lutheran congregation in Clyde organized in 1870, and bought the frame church from the Universalists for $1,900 in 1901. The church was torn down to make room for the current stone church, which was dedicated in 1927 in the same location. (Ohio History Connection.)

# Six
# A Walk Down Main Street

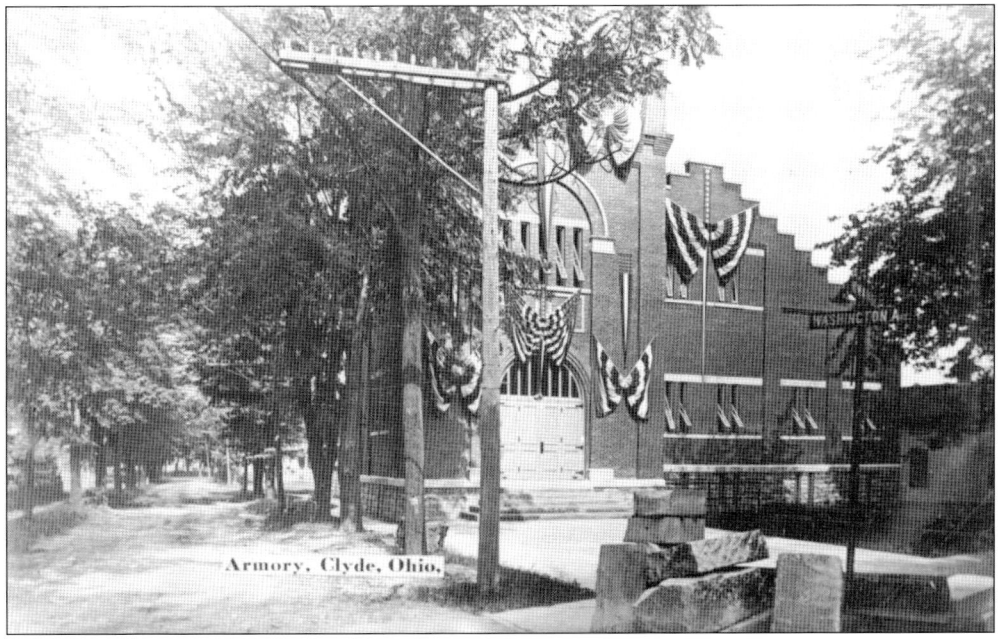

The Ohio National Guard Armory was built in 1912 at the corner of Main Street and Washington Avenue. Capt. A.H. Wicks purchased the land from the Christy family in 1910 on behalf of the Ohio State Armory Board. Local resident B.A. Becker donated $3,500 to facilitate the purchase and construction, Clyde residents raised an additional $1,500, and the State Armory Board spent $20,000. It was the first armory in the state to be located outside of a county seat. The armory was home to Ohio National Guard Company 1, 6th Infantry. Following the end of World War I, the unit was decommissioned. The company was reassembled in 1922, this time as Company 1, 148th Infantry, and included 2 officers and 48 men. In 1982, the Ohio General Assembly approved the sale of the armory, and it was decommissioned. Since then, the building has hosted baccalaureate and graduation ceremonies and dances and now houses the Erlin Trader. In 1999, Dan and Valerie Durbin bought the Erlin Trader from founder Melvin Osmun. (John Sanford.)

At one time, grain elevators were stationed along Main Street near the railroad tracks. Both of these views are looking south along Main Street. The above postcard is undated and shows Main Street from the location of today's McPherson Highway. The below image is dated February 24, 1905, and shows Main Street in a view looking south from Railroad Street, just slightly south of the vantage point in the above photograph. The Comstock & Slessman Lakeshore Elevator was built in 1895 and co-owned by Ira Comstock and George Slessman, who later established the Clyde Kraut Company together. Comstock was born in 1863 and graduated from Clyde High School. He was known throughout the midwestern United States as a "grain man" and died in 1912 at age 49. Over the course of his life, he lived in nearby York Township, served as a county commissioner, and was one of the original partners of the Farmers and Traders Bank (later the Clyde Savings Bank). His business partner, Slessman, was born in nearby Seneca County in 1853 and was very active in local politics. He served two terms as county sheriff "with the greatest efficiency in an office which carries great responsibilities with it," according to Basil Meek's *Twentieth Century History of Sandusky County, Ohio and Representative Citizens*, published in 1909. (Both, Randy Dick.)

This view of Main Street looking north from around Buckeye Street is packed with action and details of how the streetscape looked during the early 20th century. Horses and wagons are sharing the street with automobiles, while shopkeepers and customers mingle on the sidewalk. A streetlight hangs in the center of the photograph, while a florist's sign and a mounted clock are prominent in the left foreground. Hitching posts are visible in the right foreground. In the distance, the railroad tracks are visible, along with homes and a painted sign. (John Sanford.)

A boy stands in the roadway in this undated view of Main Street looking south from the railroad tracks. The Office Block building, with the people standing in front of it, housed C.W. McGuire, MD. These buildings are still standing today, with longtime residents including the Red Arrow Saloon, Dewey & Dewey law offices, and the *Clyde Enterprise*. Note the railroad crossing sign at far left, as well as the horse and carriage at right. (John Sanford.)

On February 14, 1909, a severe sleet storm struck most of northern Ohio, with Clyde, neighboring Fremont, and most of the rest of Sandusky County sustaining severe damage. Local historian Basil Meek described a storm with rain, sleet, and snow that "was undoubtedly the worst this locality has ever suffered, and broke the record of all the great ice or sleet storms that ever visited the place." These views of Main Street, one showing North Main Street (below) and one showing downtown (above), offer evidence of the damage that the storm caused. Meek recalled how "the cracking of broken limbs, the snapping of wires and breaking of the poles could be heard in all sections of the [county]." A notation on the back of one of the postcards warns the recipient that the sender is "unavoidably delayed" because of the damage. (Both, Randy Dick.)

The current Clyde City Hall building, located at 222 North Main Street, was dedicated in 1979. The larger building allowed for city offices and the police and fire departments to be housed in one building. City offices and services have since outgrown this building and now occupy additional structures in the city. (Randy Dick.)

The People's Bank was located on the northwest corner of the intersection of Main and Buckeye Streets. The building was completed in 1912 and was made of granite and pressed brick. The People's Bank was not the first bank in Clyde, but it was one of the most successful. It was established in Clyde in 1884 with capital stock of $50,000. The founding officers were John Lemmon, president; Carmi Sanford, Thomas P. Dewey, Taylor Fuller, and T.P. Hurd, vice presidents; and John Bolinger, cashier. (John Sanford.)

Main Street is bustling in this undated view looking south from Maple Street. There are horses and wagons lining the street and people sitting on benches. In the southeast corner (left in the photograph), there is a shoe store with a large clock outside, while a sign for the "Clyde Bicycle Store" is prominent. On the northwest corner (right foreground), the building that would eventually house the Big Four Restaurant is visible. It was torn down in 1967. In the next block, Hurd's Grocery is open for business. Hurd's Grocery was one of Clyde's longest-operating businesses; it opened in 1854 and closed in 1968. (Randy Dick.)

This picture of Main Street appears to have been taken from a second-floor window with a view looking north near the intersection of Main and Buckeye Street. Wilson's clothing store is visible across the street. The Lakeshore Elevator, formerly the Slessman and Comstock elevator, is prominent down the street. Note the railcar between the buildings, adjacent to the elevator. At far left, a sign for "Dewey Lawyer" is visible, and locals may recognize that the Dewey law office is still there and conducting business today. (Clyde Museum.)

This view of Main Street looking south from Buckeye Street provides a look at a historical time in Clyde's downtown. The buildings that line the block along the west side of the street are still there today, though details may have changed in their current appearances. (John Sanford.)

Horse-drawn wagons line Main Street in this undated photograph. The view appears to be looking south from near the intersection of Buckeye Street. The hardware store and Hurd's Grocery are visible at right. The utility poles are prominent. (Clyde Museum.)

Citizens began digging out downtown Clyde on November 10, 1913, following a snowstorm that is now known as the Great Lakes Storm of 1913. The "White Hurricane," or "Big Blow," was a blizzard with hurricane-force winds that slammed the Great Lakes region of the United States and Ontario, Canada, from November 7 to November 10. It remains the deadliest and most destructive storm ever to hit the area, resulting in the deaths of 250 people and the loss of 19 ships on the Great Lakes. The city of Clyde received approximately 20 inches of snow during the storm. The *Clyde Enterprise* reported that "the street committee had a force of men at work on Main Street all day Monday, removing the drifts so that teams could get through." (Both, Randy Dick.)

These two pictures of wagons from Union Delivery making deliveries along Main Street provide windows into some of the day-to-day happenings during the early 20th century. The above photograph is dated October 1910, while the below photograph is undated. Union Delivery was a delivery service from nearby Fostoria, Ohio, that would dispatch merchandise to Clyde from Fostoria merchants. In addition to the shipment teams, note the men standing outside the clearly visible storefronts in the above image. The awnings are rolled up, the building on the right has shutters, and a streetlight hangs in the distance. The unpaved (or in need of repaving) street surface is prominent below. (Above, Randy Dick; below, Clyde Heritage League Museum.)

This postcard requires a close look: a technician is at work atop of a telephone pole as shoppers conduct business below him in downtown Clyde. The image appears to have been taken from approximately Buckeye Street with a view looking south down Main Street. There were at least two active telephone companies in the city of Clyde in the beginning of the 20th century. The Clyde Telephone Company was organized and growing by 1901, and the Farmers Telephone

Company was organized in 1903 with 100 subscribers. The Clyde Telephone Company made industry headlines in 1920 when the trade journal *Telephony* reported that a "Leich magneto-multiple 800-line switchboard" had been installed. City officials were "very well pleased with the new board" and reported it "satisfactory in every respect." (John Sanford.)

Benjamin McHugh (on the right in the doorway), owner of the Metropolitan Saloon on Main Street, stands with two other men at the door of the saloon in this undated postcard. McHugh's saloon was located at 215 North Main Street and is listed in both the 1908 and 1913 Clyde city directories. Note the icicles hanging from the awnings and the snow on the ground. (Clyde Museum.)

Winfield Adare (1856–1932) stands in front of his men's clothing and home goods store, which was located at 112 South Main Street during the early 20th century. Note the displays in the store windows and the streetlight visible in the photograph. Adare ran a very successful business and served the community in a variety of positions, including as mayor and as a trustee for Clyde Savings Bank. He is buried in McPherson Cemetery. (Clyde Museum.)

The Clyde Post Office moved into its current building on Buckeye Street in 1938. Prior to the move, from 1907 to 1938, the post office was located in the first floor of this building on the southeast corner of the intersection of Main and Forest Streets. The building anchored the Economy Block, which was constructed in 1897 by George Richards, who operated a dry goods store in the building. When the block was completed in 1897, it opened to fanfare, with a local orchestra providing music. The *Clyde Enterprise* reported townspeople criticizing the block because "it projects further into the street than any other block on Main Street." The neighboring Clyde Christian Church bought the "old post office" in 1961 and demolished the building to make space for a new education center, which now occupies the site. (John Sanford.)

This postcard presents an aerial view looking north along Main Street in the 1940s and shows the Harkness Block along the west side of the street. The image shows tremendous details of downtown Clyde at that time: The architectural elements of the Harkness Block and buildings along the street are highlighted. The awnings are prominent on the storefronts, parking is not parallel, and globe lights line the street. Signage is visible for "J.C. Farrar," which longtime residents may recognize as a shoe store. Other signs advertise for a Masonic lodge on the second floor of the block, an ice-cream and candy shop, a billiards hall, a hardware and paint store, and a pharmacy. Signage is also visible for taverns in the northern block. The north end of Main Street appears more tree-lined here than it does today, and some of these buildings have been torn down. (John Sanford.)

This postcard presents the east side of Main Street, with a view looking south on August 6, 1941. The old post office is visible in the distance, while period signs mark "Shoes" and "Frigidaire." The Clyde Savings Bank is the only storefront without an awning. The bank storefront entrance is secured with a wrought-iron fence, suggesting that this photograph was taken sometime outside of business hours. Traffic is moderate, and there are a few pedestrians. Details from the west side of the street are visible via a close examination of the photograph. South Main Street is not entirely visible, but it appears that more trees lined the street then than are on it today. (Randy Dick.)

This view of Main Street in the 1940s starts at Forest Street and looks north. Old city hall is visible on the left with a prominent awning. A police car, probably from the Clyde Police Department, is parked along the west side of the street. Business signage includes "Hardware & Paint," "Ice Cream," and "Rugs." The J.W. Beck Tar Company is visible next to city hall. (Clyde Museum.)

American Candy Kitchen, located on Main Street, was managed first by John Dumit, then, after 1910, by H.K. Leidy—both of nearby Tiffin, Ohio. According to a remembrance published in the *Clyde Enterprise* in 1988, "Many Clydites have fond memories of Leidy's confectionary shop, where one could get a banana split made with a banana topped by three generous scoops of ice cream, a variety of toppings, whipped cream, nuts, and a cherry, for only 25¢." (John Sanford.)

The Heslet Dancing Academy was located on the upper floor of the Economy Block building at the corner of Main and Forest Streets and was torn down in 1961 to make room for an addition to the Clyde Christian Church. Will Heslet was the manager of the dancing school and hosted an annual "mask ball" event for his clients. This postcard is from 1911. Ina Adare Turley (1884–1929) was a talented ragtime pianist, and John Friedley was another local musician. (John Sanford.)

Ed Aldrich sits atop a white horse on Main Street. This view is looking south toward Forest Street. The old city hall and a local cobbler's building are visible in the background. (Clyde Museum.)

These two postcards show Main Street in views looking north from approximately Forest Street. The old city hall is visible at left in both views, with its prominent wrought-iron balcony. The Economy Block, which housed the post office, is visible in the below postcard. The small cobbler shop that once stood next to city hall is also visible. Note the shoppers walking along and at least one horse and wagon among the automobiles. The awnings on the storefronts were much more widespread in the time before air-conditioning. Note the utility poles and streetlights in each view. (Above, Randy Dick; below, Paula Renfro.)

The residential section of South Main Street is visible in this undated postcard. The old post office is visible at left. The old city hall is visible at right with its original wrought-iron balcony. There are also several horses and wagons in the photograph, and tall trees and utility poles line the street. (John Sanford.)

A contemporary postcard of Main Street with a view looking north from approximately Forest Street presents an updated, familiar view from the late 20th century. The balcony was removed from city hall, many of the awnings have disappeared, and parking is now parallel to traffic. (Randy Dick.)

This contemporary postcard features a close-up of Clyde's first city hall, which was located on Main Street near the intersection with Forest Street. It opened in 1882 and housed the mayor's quarters, the fire department trucks, the police department, and a concrete jail cell. The council meeting room was on the second floor. In 1979, the building was abandoned when city offices moved into the new city hall down the street. The Clyde Heritage League took over the building and renamed it Heritage Hall. A local legend claims that the gold eagle on top of the weather vane inspired Sherwood Anderson to name the newspaper in *Winesburg, Ohio* the *Winesburg Eagle*. (Randy Dick.)

Clyde Christian Church is located at 206 South Main Street. The congregation began as a small band of Disciples of Christ members led by Chella Hutchinson and began meeting in private homes around Clyde in 1905. In 1909, the members acquired a house on West Forest Street across from the Presbyterian church and began holding worship services there. At that time, the congregation included approximately 70 people. In 1926, the congregation bought the church building from the Baptist Brotherhood, then completely remodeled it. Local resident George Rhode wired the church for electricity. Clyde Christian Church was dedicated in 1927 and features a cross-gabled roof, a decorated tower, and elaborate stained-glass windows. The chancel inside the church was remodeled in 1952 with a new pulpit, baptistry, and pipe organ. In 1963, the church bought the Economy Block on the corner of Main and Forest Streets, which contained the old post office, and razed the building to make space for a new fellowship hall and education unit. (Randy Dick.)

The Eliza Ramsey Home, located at 430 South Main Street in Clyde, opened in 1926 as an "old ladies' home." It was established with a $50,000 gift from Cleveland resident Burt Ramsey in memory of his mother, who lived in Clyde and died in 1925. The home was designed by local architect Thaddeus Hurd and constructed by Leon Woodworth, who erected the Clyde Public Library. Today, the home provides residential hospice care as part of a local health network. (Randy Dick.)

Main Street, Clyde, Ohio.

These two views of South Main Street in wintertime show a tree-lined, quiet street. The below postcard is dated December 25, 1906, and shows how dense the trees that lined this section of Clyde's downtown were at one time. Homes are visible through the trees on both postcards. A single streetlight strung across the street is clearly visible, and a couple of wagons are in the distance in the below image. (Above, Randy Dick; below, Clyde Museum.)

# Index

Adair, Winfield, 27, 113
Amanda Street, 37, 38
Anderson, Karl, Sherwood, and family, 20
baseball teams, 91, 95
Bechler's General Store, 77, 84
Buckeye Street, 23–28, 60, 92–94
bus terminal, 77
Camp Fire, Clyde chapter, 91
Camp Grand, 78, 79
Cherry Street, 30
Clyde Auto Sales, 41
Clyde Christian Church, 123
Clyde City Hall, 108, 120–122
Clyde Cooperage Company, 44
Clyde Cutlery Company, 64–66
Clyde High School, 85, 87–89
Clyde Junior High School, 85, 87
Clyde Kraut Company, 50–54
Clyde Post Office, 23, 27, 45, 115, 117, 120–123
Clyde Public Library, 92–94
Clyde Tourist Camp, 80, 81
Clydesdale Motor Truck Company, 61
Eliza Ramsey Home, 124
Elmore Manufacturing Company, 55–59
Empire House Hotel, 70
Ess's Restaurant, 47
First Presbyterian Church, 97
Forest Street, 29, 30, 102
Grace Episcopal Church, 99
Hall, Lois Smila, 34
Hughes Granite Company, 48, 49
Hunter Tool Company, 46
interurban station, 73
Kistler general store, 43, 73
Kreb Commercial Car Company, 60
Main Street, 103–125
McPherson Cemetery, 11–18
McPherson, James B., 11–13
Meek, George Burton, 16
Methodist Episcopal church, 100, 101
Nichols House, 66, 69
Ohio National Guard armory, 103

People's Bank, 108
Pickett family, 62, 63
Prentice family, 39, 43, 101
railroad depot, 45, 71
Russell, Stella, 33
72nd Ohio Volunteer Infantry, 21
Smith's Restaurant, 47
St. Mary's Catholic Church, 98, 99
St. Paul's Lutheran Church, 29, 93, 102
Union School, 85, 86
Vine Street School, 85, 87
Wales, James Albert, 15
waterworks, 89
weather events, 28, 30, 38, 90, 106, 107, 111, 125
Weston Edward Payson, 22
Whirlpool, 67, 68
White Street, 40
Young, Rodger, 18

# About the Clyde Museum

The Clyde Museum is located at 124 West Buckeye Street in the former Grace Episcopal Church. The museum was established in 1931 and tells the story of Clyde, its place in Ohio, and its place in national history. The museum is operated by the Clyde Heritage League. The church was built in 1886, the museum opened in the space in 1987, and additions have expanded the space. Exhibits range from natural history and pioneer dioramas, Clyde–Green Springs Schools ephemera, and a Sherwood Anderson section. Military collections honor veterans including James B. McPherson, George Burton Meek, Charles McCleary, and Rodger Young. The museum also houses a 1904 Elmore car, a 1921 Clydesdale fire truck, a Clyde Cutlery collection, and other manufacturing artifacts.

The Clyde Museum is free and accessible to the public. The museum is open on Thursdays from 1:00 p.m. to 4:00 p.m., and it may be reached at (419) 547-7946 or at the e-mail address clydeheritageleague@yahoo.com. Find the Clyde Museum on Facebook to keep up with local history right in your newsfeed.

# Discover Thousands of Local History Books Featuring Millions of Vintage Images

Arcadia Publishing, the leading local history publisher in the United States, is committed to making history accessible and meaningful through publishing books that celebrate and preserve the heritage of America's people and places.

Find more books like this at
**www.arcadiapublishing.com**

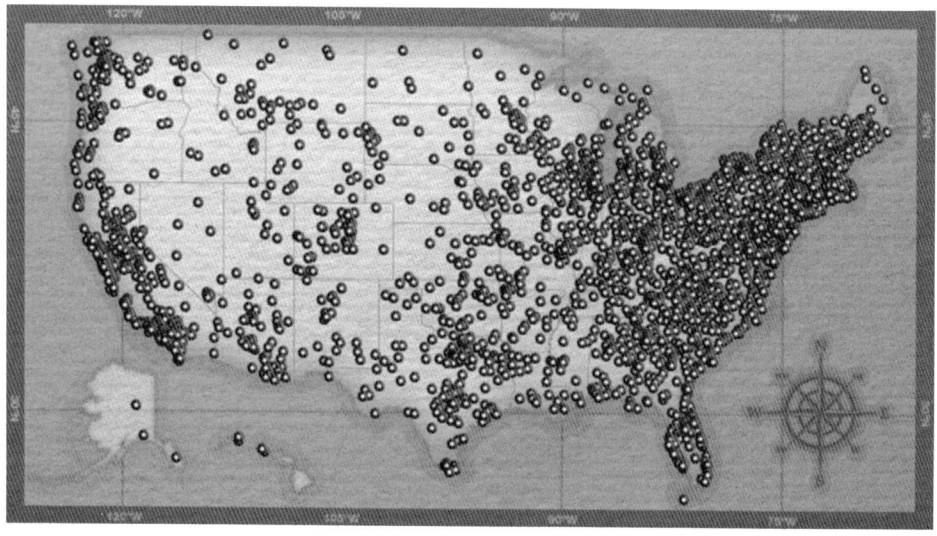

Search for your hometown history, your old stomping grounds, and even your favorite sports team.

Consistent with our mission to preserve history on a local level, this book was printed in South Carolina on American-made paper and manufactured entirely in the United States. Products carrying the accredited Forest Stewardship Council (FSC) label are printed on 100 percent FSC-certified paper.